I0201193

PALACE OF
BROKEN DREAMS

A Brief History of
Beechworth Asylum

ASYLUM
GHOST TOURS
Beechworth, Victoria
www.asylumghosttours.com

PALACE OF BROKEN DREAMS
A Brief History of Beechworth Asylum

© 2017 Asylum Ghost Tours
www.asylumghosttours.com

ISBN: 978-1-925623-23-9

Research – Dawn Roach
Compilation – Geoff Brown
Cover and Interior Design – Geoff Brown
Cover Image – Andrew Spedding

Photographers:
Andrew Spedding, Leah Roach, David Roach,
Dawn Roach, Danni Townsend-O'Neil.

Some photos and floorplans sourced from
the State Library of Victoria and the
Public Record Office, Victoria.

ALL RIGHTS RESERVED

No part of this publication may be reproduced, distributed, or
transmitted in any form or by any means, including photocopying,
recording, or other electronic or mechanical methods, without
the prior written permission of the publisher, except in the case
of brief quotations embodied in critical reviews and certain other
noncommercial uses permitted by copyright law. For permission
requests, contact the publisher at the website below.

www.asylumghosttours.com
Mayday Hills Asylum, Beechworth

Orders by trade bookstores and wholesalers through Ingram
or direct from the publisher: **asylum@cohesionpress.com**

CONTENTS

TOURS RUN THROUGH THE OLD ASYLUM
NEARLY EVERY DAY OF THE YEAR.

- AFTER DARK HISTORY/GHOST TOURS EVERY NIGHT -
- FAMILY-FRIENDLY TWILIGHT TOURS FRI& SAT -
- PURE HISTORY EVERY SATURDAY & SUNDAY -
- PRIVATE TOURS AVAILABLE ON QUERY -

ASYLUM
GHOST TOURS
BEECHWORTH, VICTORIA
0473 376 848
WWW.ASYLUMGHOSTTOURS.COM

INTRODUCTION

Beechworth Asylum has been known by many names over its 150-year history.

It was one of three Victorian asylums contracted and built in the second half of the 1800s as a result of the clear need of the government to have adequate facilities in which to place those poor people who needed constant care due to mental illness or infirmity yet were unsuited for placement in gaols, which seemed to be the common outcome at that time.

Yarra Bend Asylum, the only existing asylum facility in Victoria in the early 1800s, opened on October 5th, 1848. It began as a separate ward of Tarban Asylum in NSW, built to accommodate those patients in the region later to become Victoria, and was originally known as the 'Lunatic Asylum, Merri Creek'. After Victoria officially separated from New South Wales, the institution became Yarra Bend Asylum.

In 1852, an enquiry was held into the conditions in which people were being held at Yarra Bend, and the conclusions of the enquiry shed light on the everyday abuses of human rights and the mismanagement that characterised the asylum. Two years later, in 1854, a second enquiry recommended the construction of a new asylum to replace Yarra Bend. Another site in what is now Melbourne's inner suburbs was chosen, elevated due to the Victorian Era belief that heights and fresh air could help blow the 'lunacy' from people's minds. This new asylum, Willsmere, became one of three eventually contracted and built in the 1860s.

Willsmere would not hold enough patients, so Beechworth and Ararat were chosen to receive new asylums as well. Ararat Asylum was built and opened at roughly the same time as Beechworth Asylum.

Beechworth had been chosen as the site for the asylum over Wangaratta, which was thought to be too flood-prone. Beechworth's cause was also advanced by the efforts of its local member, George Briscoe Kerferd, who later became the Victorian premier of the time.

The decision to locate the new asylum at Beechworth was made in May 1864, following which the Government surveyor arrived in the town to select the site. Of a possible three, the eventual site was chosen for its elevated aspect and its potential for expansion.

The asylum was initially constructed as the Beechworth Lunatic Asylum between 1864 and 1867 by contractor Abraham Linacre, probably to the design of Public Works Department architect JJ Clark. It is said the majority of labouring was carried out by hard-labour prisoners from HM Prison Beechworth, situated only 1500 metres from the asylum. Many of the buildings erected around the grounds and used in connection with the asylum farm were built using asylum labour. Sometimes the materials for these structures were supplied by the Department, but in other cases, it was obtained locally. About 3,250,000 bricks were reported to have been used in the course of the project. About 250,000 feet of hardwood was used and this was sawn on-site using the same plant used to grind the clay for the bricks.

Both the bricks and timber were transported by means of a wooden tramway.

The buildings from this early period are cement rendered, one-, two- and three-storeyed Italianate-style structures set within what is now an extensive parkland containing mature exotic and native trees and remnants of the original encircling 'ha-ha' wall. The main asylum building features covered verandahs, walkways and airing courts typical of asylums from the era in which it was built. The verandahs were supported by three hundred and fifty tubular iron posts, which also acted as pipes to convey water from the roof into the cisterns around the yard. The main facility, built in the shape of a capital E if viewed from overhead, opened for inmates on October 24th, 1867.

The facility was quickly filled to capacity, and maybe beyond. The first group of patients were led in a procession along Albert Road to the top of the formerly triple-peaked area known as Mayday Hills. An enduring theme in the history of the Beechworth institution has been its struggle to make do with the accommodation on the site. Nineteenth century Inspector's Reports provide a list of the ongoing works requirements. Many of the maintenance and repair works could be carried out by the patients themselves, but there was a constant pressure on facilities as the number of patients requiring care rose in the late nineteenth century. Indeed, the pressure on the Lunacy Department was such that additions were required at Beechworth within a few years of its construction.

By the end of 1868, the number of patients at beechworth had reached close to 300. The inadequate nature of the services at the complex was also an ongoing concern for its administrators, particularly as the numbers of patients rose dramatically in the 1890s.

Prior to the opening, the patients had been held in the Old Beechworth Gaol, and the grand procession left the gaol to walk (or, in some cases, be carried) to the asylum at approximately 2.30 in the afternoon. The first patient death occurred the next day, October 25th 1867. The gentleman in question, Mr John Whitehead (or Whitehouse, as the records are unclear) was gravely ill when he was carried up to the asylum on a litter borne by two other patients.

INQUEST AT THE LUNATIC ASYLUM

An inquest was held yesterday at the Beechworth Lunatic Asylum touching the death of one of the inmates named John Whitehead, or Whitehouse, nobody knew which was his real name. [The] deceased had been admitted on Friday afternoon from the gaol, amongst the first batch of

FRONT GATE HM GAOL BEECHWORTH

insane patients. He was in a hopeless state, and died on Saturday. The inquest was held before Mr Butler, coroner, and a jury of twelve. One of the jury asked Dr Dick, one of the witnesses examined, whether the removal had probably accelerated [the deceased's] death. Dr Dick thought not. Dr Dempster deposed to [the] deceased having died from disease of the brain, and the jury returned a verdict accordingly.

— Ovens & Murray Advertiser, 29th Oct 1867, p2

On admittance, the patients were put to work in the facility according to any qualifications or skills they held and their ability to work. Blacksmithing, carpentry, painting and further building works, tailoring and shoemaking, hairdressing: all tasks within the asylum were performed by inmates as far as possible. The farming areas were filled with patient labourers, too. Everyone who was able to do so earnt their keep.

The women, for there were female patients as well, would work as domestic servants, seamstresses, weavers, laundry workers, and anything else that required the keen eye and delicate touch of a woman.

Records show that recreational activities were increased from the 1880s, coinciding with an influx of new patients in the same period. Within a few years of opening, the facility grew overcrowded and unable to house the increasing numbers of patients being brought in.

Two more buildings were added onto the original building (one on the male side, the other on the female side) in 1873. With the two additions, the asylum offered nineteen dormitories and nine day-rooms.

Gas lighting was first introduced to the asylum in the mid-1880s, allowing the nights to be more warm and welcoming inside the wardrooms, dining areas, and common areas.

THE PINES WARD - COMMON SLEEPING AREA

The detached cottages at the eastern edge of the facility were constructed around the same time, with records showing completion through the mid-to-late 1880s, bringing the capacity of the asylum up to between 500 and 600 patients. The staff grew at the same time, with the single and shared staff cottages in front of the main western aspect of the façade becoming more and more unsuitable to the task of housing the extra nursing and administration staff required to run such a large and growing facility.

In the first two decades of the twentieth century, Mayday Hills significantly expanded and upgraded its facilities. New buildings constructed in this period included a variety of farm structures, which were built by the patients at the hospital, as well as two substantial Public Works Department-designed buildings. These were new mess rooms for the attendants and nurses (1906) and a new superintendent's house (1908). Two of the cottages were linked as part of their conversion to a hospital and infirmary.

Sporting facilities were expanded in the grounds, with establishment in 1911 of a bowling green and a tennis court in the two courtyards. The pavilion near the main entrance was erected around the same time. The involvement of the Lunacy Department's landscape architect, Hugh Linaker, saw improvement works to the ornamental garden.

The nurses' quarters and the ward now known as Turquoise were built to the design of Public Works Department architect Percy Everett in 1936. In the post-war era the treatment of the mentally ill underwent radical change and many buildings were added to the hospital and earlier buildings modernised.

The Fire of '51

The fire that destroyed part of the male wing in 1951 called for some serious remodelling of the affected areas. What was a long, single two-storey wing became a series of one and two-storey areas that are linked by the surviving verandahs. The fire, seemingly a result of wiring shorting out in the attic space on the male side, led to the evacuation of several hundred patients, with only one injury as a result. The injury was a male attendant who broke a collarbone falling off the verandah while helping patients down to the ground.

The patients were given living space in the central hall, in the Beechworth Town hall, and also in various homes of staff and Beechworth locals who all leapt at the chance to help where they could. Later, many patients were transferred to other asylum and hospital facilities.

The asylum remodelled the affected areas and life went back to normal.

THE MAIN ASYLUM

B eechworth Asylum, and those at Kew (Willsmere), and Ararat (Aradale) were all designed to follow the administration and treatment concepts as written in John Conolly's *The Construction and Government of Lunatic Asylums and Hospitals for the Insane* (1847)

Conolly's proposed methods of treatment reflected the reform of psychiatric care in the Victorian period, away from practices such as restraints and towards a more dignified consideration and treatment of the 'lunatic' as a mentally-unwell person.

Beechworth Asylum has had four official names and one overriding colloquial name throughout its 128 years of operation.

1867: Beechworth Lunatic Asylum opened October 24th
1905: Renamed Beechworth Hospital for the Insane
1934: Renamed Beechworth Mental Hospital (1934–1995)
1964: Beechworth Training Centre (1964–1995)
1970: Renamed Beechworth Mental/Psychiatric Hospital
1995: Decommissioned

The asylum facility is architecturally significant as a particularly fine example of an extensive complex of Italianate asylum buildings dating from the 1860s, and in the case of the cottages, the 1880s. The design is based on the influential asylum at Colney Hatch in England and shares many features in common with other contemporary institutions, notably Willsmere in Kew and Aradale at Ararat, both constructed as part of the same move to house those considered mentally unwell in large institutions. It displays key characteristic features such as the E-shaped plan of the main administration, kitchen and dormitory block with its airing courts and covered walkways, as well as the

FRONT ADMINISTRATION BUILDING - THE BIRCHES

gatehouse, mortuary and ha-ha wall. The restrained design of the 1860s buildings is attributed to the important Public Works Department architect, JJ Clark.

Mayday Hills Hospital is historically and socially important for its physical manifestation of the changing approaches to the treatment of mental illness in Victoria from institutional confinement to treatment and rehabilitation, and from barracks, through cottages to wards.

Beechworth Asylum has been crucially important in the social history of Beechworth and has, along with the gaol, contributed significantly to the economic viability and survival of this historically-important town. Its size and prominent siting have had an important and long lived social and economic impact on the town and region.

Beechworth Asylum and its landscaped garden setting is aesthetically important for the beauty of its picturesque setting on a prominent hill among extensive parklands made up of native and introduced trees and shrubs.

છ ૐ ૹ

HISTORICAL BACKGROUND

The site for the Beechworth Asylum was reserved in 1864 following the decision a year earlier to erect two large new asylums in country Victoria, one at Ararat and the other at Beechworth. Government contractor Mr Abraham Linacre's tender of £80,000 was accepted and work started on 16 December 1865, although the final cost of the lodges, workshops, sunken wall and furniture was £107,982. The Asylum opened on October 24th 1867, incorporated a large farm, a vegetable garden, and extensive ornamental grounds.

The 1905 Cyclopedia of Victoria described the hospital as ". . . the only really imposing building in Beechworth". The article goes on to further describe the hospital and its routine: "The Hospital for the Insane is built on the top of a hill, and is surrounded by extensive grounds, which are cultivated by the inmates themselves, under the supervision of the warders. The institution is capable of accommodating between 500 and 600 inmates, and, besides the immense wards necessitated by so large a number, several cottages have been erected to accommodate twenty-five patients in each. The cottages are for the use of the old and harmless lunatics. The work of the institution is performed almost entirely by the patients themselves, who are taken care of by male and female warders. There is a fine concert hall, adapted for theatrical or musical performances, where entertainments are given, at which the more harmless patients assist. This hall was artistically painted and decorated by one of the wardens, who also painted several sets of scenery, but it has since been retouched by one of the patients."

The complex continued to function as a psychiatric hospital until the late 20th century. In 1938, the Wangaratta Ladies Auxiliary formed, and community members took an active role contributing to patients' comforts and interests. In 1952, the Mental Health Authority established the 'Open Door' policy, demolishing the perimeter wall in 1955 and allowing the patients much more freedom.

GATHERING IN FRONT OF THE ADMIN BUILDING - 1920S?

By the 1960s, a Nurse Training School and adjacent Nurses' Home had been established at the hospital, leading to major developments in nursing education.

In 1962, the Mental Retardation and Mental Hospital sections were officially separated. In 1964, several wards were renovated, renamed and re-opened as a Training Centre specifically to care for and train more than 200 people with intellectual disabilities.

In 1977, the psychiatric hospital was proclaimed, and renamed as such, under the *Mental Health Act 1959*. In the late 1980s and early 1990s, the development of other residential options (day placements, education, employment, and recreational opportunities) meant there were fewer clients.

By 1992, all intellectual-disability clients had been removed from the hospital and placed in other forms of accommodation. By 1993, the psychiatric hospital had a capacity of 130 beds, with only twenty available for acute adult patients and more than seventy for geriatric patients.

By the mid-90s, the hospital consisted of two psychogeriatric wards (Emerald and Amethyst), the Kerferd Acute Clinic, Willow, and external housing at Gilchrest Avenue and Mayday Court. The process of decommissioning was underway and that year the site was added to the *Register of Historic Buildings*.

The Beechworth Psychiatric Hospital was finally decommissioned in 1995, when so many similar facilities in Victoria underwent the same process.

La Trobe University paid $750,000 for the heritage-listed facility a year later in 1996, then went on to use the site as a hotel and conference centre to teach hospitality and tourism courses. La Trobe continued to use sections of the facility until 2011, and then sold on to private owners in 2013. The new owners, two local businessmen who are passionate about ensuring the facility lives on, are leasing and selling sections to tourism operators and arts-based businesses, as well as making a few of the smaller buildings available for private purchase for residential purposes.

The former Mayday Hills Hospital is set on a hill, south-east of the commercial centre of Beechworth and is surrounded by open farmland, hedged in part with hawthorn.

Mayday Hills is a beautiful hilltop complex consisting of many unique and varied buildings. It sits at the top of Albert Road, overlooking the historic and picturesque town of Beechworth like an old queen overlooking her kingdom, regal yet showing her age.

"Situated on the brow of a hill, about a mile to the south-east of Beechworth, at an elevation of some hundreds of feet above that township. The front faces west and commands a panoramic view of Beechworth.

"... it is intended to make the establishment, as nearly as possible, self-supporting, this land will be fenced in and cultivated, the necessary work being performed principally by pauper inmates, who are not so much affected as to, render a continual supervision necessary. Beside agriculture, provision will be made for those unfortunates who are tradesmen to ply their art, and work-shops are being erected with this end, so that a good deal of work of various descriptions will he turned out."

-- Ovens and Murray Supplement

Original boundaries of the Asylum and Farm

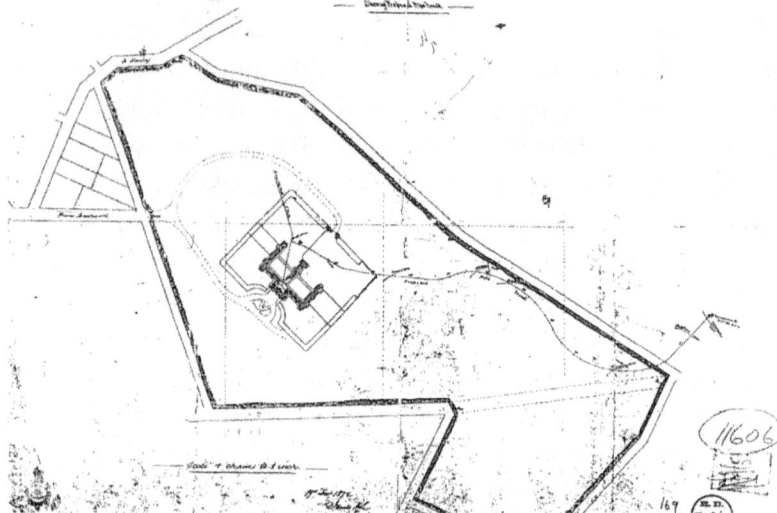

Patient Areas within the Containment (Ha-Ha) Wall

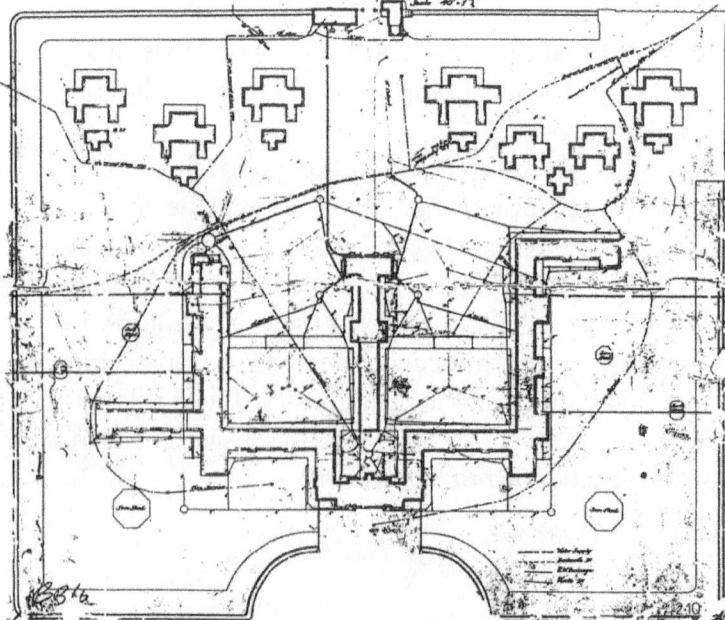

BUILDINGS STILL STANDING

The asylum grounds originally covered two hundred acres. It was nearly completely self-sufficient due to farming, orchards, vegetable gardens, and livestock. As modern supply lines came into being in the area, the lands were gradually repurposed and sold off, and the entire facility now covers less than fifty acres.

In the early years, patients who were able worked in the gardens, orchards, farm, sewing room, laundry and kitchen for their keep. Later they were paid for their labour. It was thought that working to help support themselves gave the more capable patients a sense of purpose and self-esteem. Originally only kerosene lamps and fireplaces gave light and comfort to the occupants. There are fireplaces all through the facility, mostly unusable now, and electricity was connected in 1926. The E-shaped main building was made using granite foundations and over three million handmade bricks, hand-sawn lumber, and hand-crafter nails and fasteners.

RECREATION HALL/BIJOU THEATRE COMPLEX

This two-storey hall and store complex was constructed between 1864-67 as part of the original main building, forming the centre stroke of a capital E when viewed from overhead.

It is made up of the central store area and meat cellar, the main kitchen that fed the entire asylum, and the hall itself, intended for recreational activities, concerts, and live theatre for the patients, as well as being used for nursing exams in later years of the asylum's operation. The Bijou has undergone various extensions and alterations through the years, and has been used for a variety of things, including staff library and reading rooms (westernmost end downstairs area), staff billiard room (westernmost end upstairs which later served as a pharmacy area) and the bell tower between the hall and the library.

In the early 1940s the kitchen was completely refurbished and became a foyer are for the newly-installed cinema, complete with mezzanine and projection box in the upper section.

As seen all through the facility, there are verandahs surrounding a large portion of the hall, and covered walkways joining the hall complex to the male and female wings north and south of the central hall.

COVERED WALKWAY FROM THE BIJOU THEATRE ENTRANCE
ACROSS TO THE WOMEN'S WARD/LAUNDRY AREA

The stores area in the east end of the wing comprises two large store rooms on the ground floor and rooms to the north and south originally used as female and male attendants' mess rooms respectively.

The original suspended timber floor in the west store room has been replaced with solid concrete. The fireplaces and chimney pieces in the north and south mess rooms have been removed. The south room, now an office, has been refurbished recently, and the ceiling has been replaced in plasterboard.

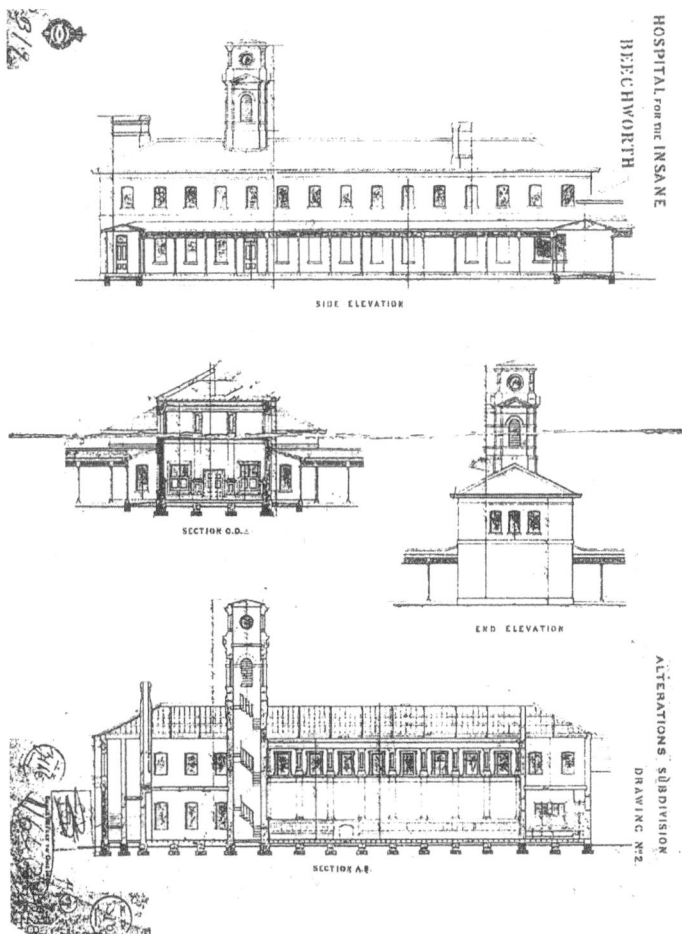

CONTRACT PLANS FOR THE BIJOU/STORE BUILDING FROM ALL FOUR ASPECTS, SHOWING THE BELL TOWER

A dumb waiter down to the basement is reported to have been removed from the lobby next to the south office.

The north mess room has a battened hardboard ceiling. This room is notable for its painted frieze, with panels on each wall depicting landscape scenes, some of which appear possibly to be of the local area.

FRIEZE IN EASTERN END OF STORE

Upon speaking to Mr Doug Craig, one of the final managers of the asylum and the author of *The Lion of Beechworth*, we were told the frieze was painted by a patient in the late 1890s.

The Store is still a major feature as first seen when entering the facility from the south edge, and appears in excellent condition. The Store was recently used as a public gallery space and studio space by the Beechworth Arts Council (BAC).

THE CELLAR

The cellar below the stores was the cold-storage area for meats and other perishables. It takes up the same area below ground level as the stores area does above.

Access was through a slide that led down for goods delivery, as well as a rope- or chain-operated wooden lift section, a dumbwaiter, in the southern edge of the Store lobby where heavier cargo could be lowered with more ease.

This was later dismanted.

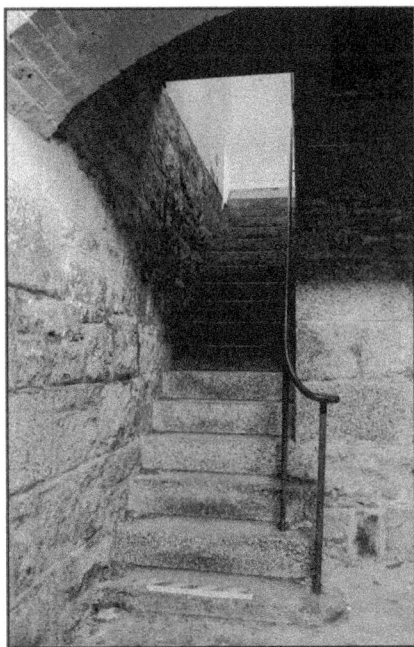

It is rumoured that the prisoners who helped build the asylum were often locked in the cells behind the metal gates instead of returning to the gaol at night, which makes sense in the amount of extra work that could be done instead of travelling. It also lowered the risk of escape attempts during the trips from gaol to the asylum. There are barred air and light wells situated on the north, south, and eastern aspects of the cellar, and there are signs of two more airwells

GATED WESTERN STORAGE AREA IN CELLAR

on the northern access that have since been filled in during the renovations that added the butcher's area to the west of the cellar. The brickwork in one of the storage rooms supports this.

The Birches (Administration Building)

EARLY POSTCARD SHOWING THE ADMIN BUILDING FACADE

The main administration building is a three-storey building situated in the front and centre of the asylum. It originally housed the superintendent, the surgeons, surgeries, and administration areas for the asylum. The administration block was constructed in 1864–67 to house both offices and meeting rooms. It appears later to have been used also for accommodation for medical staff.

The front elevation is bookended by two square Italianate towers with hipped roofs rising above the main roof and a visually separate central block with narrow set-back linking sections between the towers and the central block.

The three-storey administration block is the central part of the E-shaped main building, and is flanked on each side by the former male and female accommodation wards

The second floor is currently leased by Beechworth Day Spa, although their lease expires mid-2018 and it is expected they will move to a new facility just down the hill from the asylum.

Hospital for Insane, Beechworth

The third floor contains access to the attic on each side wing. The attics each run the length of the north and south buildings, and are rumoured to have been used to gain fast access to any area of the main building in case of emergency. The ladders that lead to the attic areas in many parts of the two wings seem to sustain that rumour.

The asylum administration block is a beautiful building, as stated in *The Ovens & Murray Advertiser* in 1903.

"It is not too much to say that the Beechworth Lunatic Asylum is the most prettily situated and the most attractive looking of any public institution in Beechworth, and this is no accident; it is a matter of deliberate design."

The article quoted above, 'A Run Through the Beechworth Lunatic Asylum' was printed on the 6th June, 1903, and allows for a more reserved and kind opinion of what the asylum is like, as a facility, for staff and patients, and what it meant to Beechworth.

ༀ ᠃ᢀ᠊ འ

WARD – WOMEN'S FRONT AKA MATRON'S AREA

This wing, where the asylum tour begins, was part of the first 1864–67 phase of construction.

WOMENS' WING - COURTYARD IN FRONT (WESTERN) AREA

The wing comprised part of the female patients' accommodation, containing dormitories and single bedrooms, day rooms and attendants' rooms. The less-noisy and more controllable patients were kept here toward the front of the asylum, while the more erratic and noisy patients were kept further east in what was known as the maniacal wing.

Part of the south-west wing has been absorbed into the central administration block, and the remainder of the wing was extensively altered in the mid-1970s for use as an occupational therapy unit on the ground floor and a nurses' training school on the first floor. There are still signs showing School of Nursing through the area.

According to town legend, Matron Sharpe, one of the early matrons for the asylum, still haunts the hallways in this area, watching over everyone to ensure things run smoothly.

Matron Sharpe is renowned for her forward-thinking introduction of art therapy, music therapy, and even pet therapy for the patients using birds in cages to provide a more pleasant environment. It would have pleased her that the local Montessori School leased the building for a few years, and that it's now being set up as the main area for the new Mayday Hills Art Society.

This section of the women's side was restored in the Twentieth Century, showing as white rendering with arched windows in good condition from the outside.

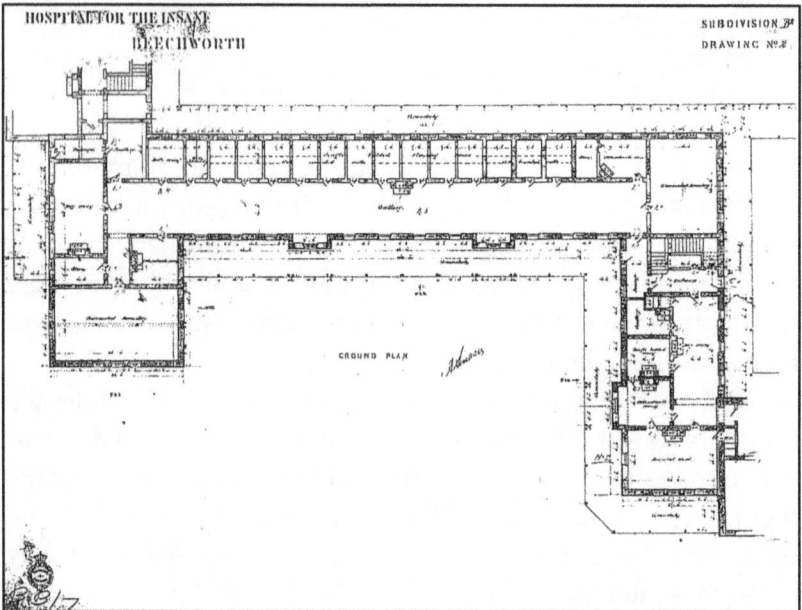

GROUND FLOOR CONTRACT PLAN FOR THE WOMEN'S WING

Of special note, the attic over the School of Nursing section holds what locals call the Hall of Fame, where new nursing staff would go up and paint their surname and starting year on the rafters in white paint. The earliest name/date combination we have found so far dated back to 1951, and the rest of the many names stretched all the way through until 1994.

WARD – WOMEN'S MANIACAL

WOMEN'S MANIACAL WARD VIEWED FROM THE CAR PARK AREA

The north-east section of the female patients' wing was constructed as part of the original 1864–67 contract. Today, this section is easily the most historically-important part of the facility due to it still retaining the most original layout of any ward in the asylum. It is the only wing in which the early pink-hued wash finish to the external render remains visible.

The most substantial alterations have been to the single storey wing at the east end. Built originally as the laundry issuing room and boiler house, it appears to have been progressively enlarged during the twentieth century to house larger heating plant and engineers' accommodation. Most of these accretions have been

PALACE OF BROKEN DREAMS

MANIACAL WING VERANDAH - SOUTH FACADE LOOKING WEST

demolished, leaving only the skillion-roofed section to the north of the original single-storey wing.

Internally, the main alterations to the plan form have been the removal of the WC compartments in the laundry, laundresses' and matrons' quarters and patients' accommodation.

The north-east women's ward, also known as the Women's Maniacal Ward, included laundry at the east end on the ground floor and a sewing section room on the first floor. A drawing dated 1867 indicates that soon after the initial building work was completed,

SEWING ROOM, EASTERN END

the east end was extensively altered and extended to provide a new boiler enclosure to the east and a small engineer's residence.

The female wing was extended in 1873 by construction of a large wing to the north. This wing was an extension of the projecting dormitory wing at the west end of the original female wing. The extension, including the original dormitory wing, was demolished in the mid-1970s. The area to the north of the women's ward now contains a 1970s ward building that is currently used for storage and some residential areas.

The laundry and boiler house sections were further altered and extended in the twentieth century. A new boiler house and a large brick chimney were constructed, probably in c. 1914, when a new boiler was installed and hot water radiator heating was installed in the female wing.

The new boiler house was later further extended. A range of brick, weatherboard and corrugated iron structures, including engineers' and blacksmiths' workshops appear to have been constructed at various dates in the twentieth century. All of these extensions have now been demolished.

The washhouse was also extended on the north side and a toilet extension within the north verandah was constructed, both of these extensions at unknown dates probably in the twentieth century.

UPPER FLOOR MANIACAL WARD - ORIGINAL CELLS

GOUGES INSIDE CELL DOOR

The Women's Maniacal Ward still contains eight original 1860s cells, with four on the ground floor and four immediately above on the first floor. The original cell doors still show the gouges and teeth marks from patients eager to get out of the cells that contained them. The windows to the cells are fitted with two-part vertically-sliding shutters mounted in full-height box frames. The cells open onto a day room with mantled fireplaces, now bricked in and covered. The upstairs mantle is still in place, although the mantle downstairs is missing.

The centre of the wing contains a small area that is rumoured to be the head matron's apartment, with a day-room south of the central passageway and a sitting room and bedroom north of the passageway. This small set of rooms was once completely isolated from the cell areas to the west and sewing rooms to the east, but later works took out the water closet (WC) and storage. This work resulted in creation of a passageway between the patients' accommodation and the remainder of the wing, which had not existed originally.

LIGHT WELL, MANIACAL WARD

UPPER FLOOR MANIACAL WING - DAY ROOM RECONSTRUCTION

The winding wooden stairway with ground floor access was the only way to gain entry to the matron's area, giving her a space near her patients yet the privacy required to live comfortably.

The ground-floor area immediately below the matron's rooms was once the seamstress' area, and its layout is identical to the matron's area above.

This wing was closed in the mid-1970s and used as storage, and is now only accessible through the tour company.

OUTSIDE LAUNDRY SECTION

LAUNDRY

The far eastern end of the women's maniacal ward housed, on the lower floor, the laundry area for the facility. Patients who were capable of helping performed many duties associated with the care and delivery of all the laundered material for the entire asylum: washing, drying, ironing, folding and storage of clothes, linen and blankets all took place in the Laundry.

The double-height ceiling and vent system allowed for the extremely hot and moist atmosphere of the working laundry processes.

LAUNDRY LANTERN,
FAR EASTERN END

WARD – MEN'S AKA THE BULL PIT
(INCLUDES GARNET AND SAPPHIRE WARDS)

MALE WARDS END AFTER FIRE OF '51

Originally attached to the main building, the south-east wing (also known colloquially as The Bullpit) now comprises two separate structures; a single-storey workshop building to the west (now a small private residence) and the L-shaped two-storey 1873 wing to the east and south.

This wing was built in two stages. The first section, forming the south-east arm of the original E-shaped building, was constructed as part of the 1864–67 phase of construction. Its eastern end was on the line of the west end wall of the existing two-storey section of the wing. In 1873, an L-shaped extension to the wing

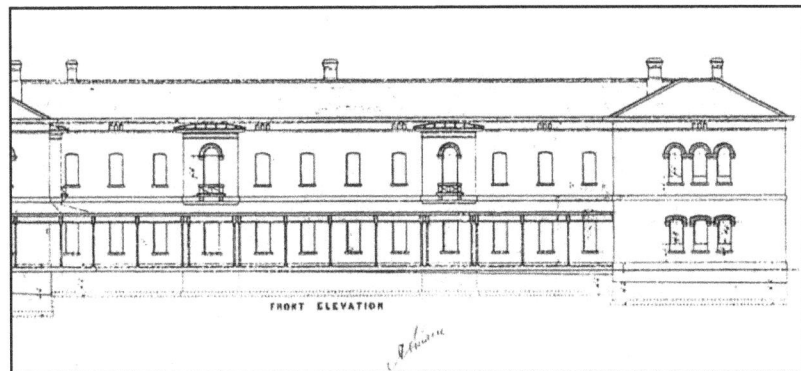

DRAWING OF WESTERN SIDE OF BULLPIT

was constructed to the east and south of the original wing. In 1936, two two-storey toilet blocks were constructed at the south end of the 1873 wing and on the south side of the 1867 wing.

The west part of the wing was damaged in the August 1951 fire, and parts were subsequently demolished. As reconstructed in 1953, the south-west corner of the wing was demolished and the eastern part of the original 1867 wing was rebuilt as a single-storey workshop detached from the 1873 wing. At the same time the 1936 toilet block next to the rebuilt workshop was reduced to one storey; the 1936 toilet block to the south end of the 1873 wing was altered and enlarged, and a new two storey toilet extension was constructed at the south-east corner of the 1873 wing.

GROUND FLOOR PLAN OF THE SOUTH-EAST MALE WING DATED 1873

The toilets in the 1873 wing were refurbished in 1979, and the workshop toilet block has been demolished. The west end wall of the 1873 wing was rebuilt in 1953 to form a new external wall.

Verandahs run along the north and east sides of the ward, still connected to the continuous line of covered walkways extending back to the administration block. A covered path connects the southeast wing with Building 33. There is a verandah on the south and west elevations between the west end wall and the projecting day room wing at the south end. The verandah is the standard cast iron columned type, with original diagonal iron strapwork frieze panels. The columns are paired in front of the projecting bay to the west elevation. A steel fire escape stair has been added to the south-east end of the wing.

Most of windows to the north elevation do not have iron glazing bar covers, and appear to have been replaced in 1953. The west and north facing windows to the projecting wing at the south-west corner and the south end wall have

GRANITE STAIRWAY BULLPIT

stilted segmental arches at ground floor level and are round-arched at first floor level. The first floor window to the projecting west elevation bay has a similar round-arched window with a console table on paired consoles and a square section wrought iron railing with diagonal cross bars.

The Bullpit is said to have been used exclusively for younger men in their teens and twenties.

The name 'Bullpit' allegedly came about from both the effect of having so many testosterone-fuelled young men in close proximity, almost like a cattle pen filled with young, virile bulls, and also from the often-told legend of staff making sure the boys/ young men were loaded with laxatives as well as having pants too big for them, a means to reduce violence between inmates.

This was said to have them concentrating so hard on holding up their pants up and getting to the toilets they were too busy to get into fights in the exercise area outside the western aspect of the ward.

80 ℓℓ ଓ

PHARMACY

The old pharmacy below the men's wards section was originally part of the male ward as well. It was lucky to have escaped the fire of 1951, as the damage to the upper part of the wing ended just before this building section. The bars on the windows in this lower area attest to the high security required where pharmaceuticals were stored.

COURTYARD AND ENTRANCE TO PHARMACY AREA

This ward wing was part of the initial 1864–67 phase of construction, and contained part of the male patients' accommodation, including a hospital, dormitories and single bedrooms, day rooms and attendants' rooms. As said earlier, the south wing was extensively damaged by the fire in August 1951. Parts of the wing were demolished as part of the reconstruction of 1953, and the central part of the wing became a separate single storey building now used as private accommodation. The north section of the wing, which remained attached to the central administration block, was remodelled as male patients' wards, and the single storey building was converted to a therapy wing.

The east part of the ground floor of the north wing was later used as a pharmacy, which was later moved into the adjacent western part. The first floor of the north section has become part of the administration offices.

TAILOR'S SHOP

Built in the 1950s, and extensively repainted and restored in the late 90s, the one-storey building was at one time leased by the Riverland Church, Beechworth.

It is now a private residence.

TOY SHOP

Originally two storeys similar to the women's ward on the opposite side of the Bijou Theatre complex (ochre-coloured render) until the fire on the 17th of August, 1951, damaged the majority of this section of the male wing.

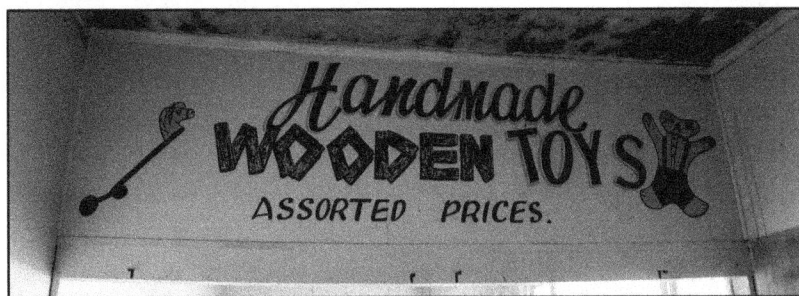

HAND-PAINTED SIGN IN OLD TOY SHOP AREA

The Toy Shop was built for the men in the years following the fire to cater for woodworking, painting and other such crafts.

Women took part in homecrafts such as needlework and embroidery.

We have heard that the products of the Toy Shop (wooden cut-out bears, toy single and two-level service stations, and other common wooden toys of the era) were sold to the public by the wives of the staff, and the funds raised were used to purchase Christmas gifts and other treats for the patients.

KIOSK

The Kiosk, formerly one of a pair, sits between the Store area and the male wing of the asylum. Built in the early 1900s to an Edwardian style, it almost resembles a small country schoolhouse. Its decorative timber detailing of half-timbered gables and exaggerated eaves brackets contrasts with the more austere style of the surrounding wards, yet still looks a cohesive part of the asylum.

KIOSK VIEWED FROM SOUTH-EASTERN ASPECT

The Kiosk was constructed to replace the original attendants' mess rooms located in the north and south wings at the east end of the centre stores wing. It provided a dining room with attached small kitchen and pantry, and a billiards room for the male attendants. The slate squares for the billiard table's legs, as well as the overhead light array to light up the table, are still evident in the second room of the Kiosk.

In the mid-1960s it became a kiosk for the patients to purchase snacks, treats, newspapers, and other such things often found in a corner shop of any town.

ଚ୍ଚ ✒ ଓଃ

CATERING CENTRE/1980S STAFF CAFETERIA

The Catering Centre, near the southern end of the main asylum grounds, was opened in 1981 after the original kitchen, situated in the Central Recreation Hall, closed. It included a cafeteria, amenities and a lounge for staff, and is thought to have been built on the grounds of a former male airing yard.

This is supported by early photos of the asylum taken from a more southern aspect.

AIRING YARDS

The two patient airing yards to either side of the hall allowed patients to get some fresh air, and to mingle. The two sides of the asylum were separated by gender in the early years.

FEMALE COURTYARD – WITH FOUNTAIN

The female airing yard later became the tennis courts (1911), and then returned to a more relaxed outdoor area complete with water fountain.

MALE COURTYARD – WITH ROTUNDA

The male airing yard was later adapted to include bowling & croquet greens (1911), and later on a small example of the kind of rotunda that was once prevalent in the ground was built. It remains today, and weddings often take place in the male courtyard.

GARDENS

The gardens surrounding the asylum buildings are listed as 'of heritage interest'. A Tree Walk pamphlet available from the George Kerferd Hotel shows the three suggested walking areas for trees and shrubs, and outlines the main plants of interest.

The gardens were created and designed by Robert Coates, a patient transferred from Yarra Bend Asylum in Melbourne (Yarra Bend was the only asylum in the state of Victoria until it was closed down after a government investigation into overcrowding and lack of care for the patients). Mr Coates was, before his commital, a landscape gardener by trade. The gardens were then maintained by patients as a form of therapy. The 1910s saw the Lunacy Department's landscape architect, Hugh Linaker, develop the gardens into what you see now.

RETAINING (HA-HA) WALL

The original retaining wall that surrounds the main asylum buildings was built just after the opening to prevent patients from escaping.

From the outside, the wall looks low while on the inside there is a trench making the walls too high to climb over.

The name is thought to originate from either half up/half down or laughing at those held behind the high side.

The wall was mostly demolished in 1955.

COTTAGE WARDS/LODGES –

A major addition to the asylum facility was made in the late 1800s in the form of construction of seven new cottages on the eastern edge of the main facility to help house a larger number of patients. All the cottages are single-storey, U-shaped brick structures. The U-shape partially surrounds a central courtyard with single rooms along the north and south arms, with a separate bathroom and laundry section along the west side. A verandah surrounds the day room area along the eastern side of each building. Of the seven new buildings, four were on the male side, and three on the female side.

CARINYA LODGE (F7)

Carinya, the northernmost cottage, was designed to hold twenty patients. In 1938, it was given over to people with an intellectual disability, who were at the time referred to as imbecile patients. It is now a private residence.

ONE OF THE COTTAGE WARDS, SHOWING VERANDAH AND GARDEN

MYRTLE/KIAMA LODGE (F6)

Like Carinya, Myrtle (name changed to Kiama during the period La Trobe owned the facility) also held twenty female patients.

Little is confirmed of the occupants in the early years, but Myrtle is said to have held the more dangerous female patients, referred to as the criminally-insane, including those who are a danger to others as well as to themselves. Staff we have spoken to have told us that in the later years of operation, Myrtle was used as a home for those who were bedridden and/or non-communicative in nature, called the profoundly handicapped. Myrtle is now a private residence and is being upgraded for short-term accommodation purposes.

KURRAJONG LODGE (M7)

On the male side, most of the cottages are a little larger, each designed to house up to thirty male patients. Kurrajong is said to have housed intellectually-disabled but harmless patients, along with those suffering from what we now call Down's Syndrome. Kurrajong is now a private residence.

GREVILLEA LODGE (M8 & M9)

One of the last of the cottages built in the 1890s, the large building we now call Grevillea was originally two cottages that were joined together in 1914 to form the male infirmary. It was turned into a mixed gender infirmary later again.

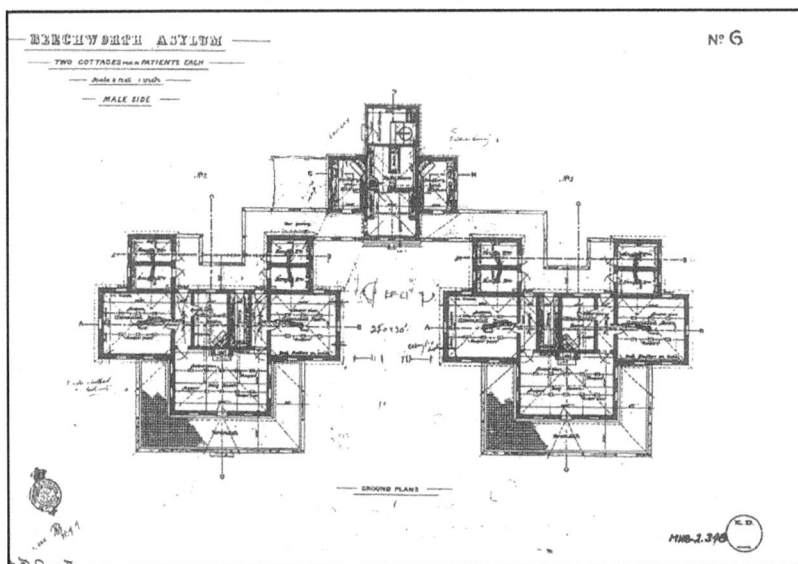

CONTRACT PLAN FOR WHAT WOULD BECOME GREVILLEA, SHOWING THE TWO SEPARATE 14-BED COTTAGES

Approximately 3,000 patients died in this building alone, due to its use as a medical and palliative care unit for the asylum.

This building was constructed in 1889-90 as two 14-patient cottages for male patients comprising an attendant room, store, two wards, a day room and single cells laid out in a U-shape. The buildings were linked at the rear (west side) by verandahs and a shared bathroom and kitchen pavilion. Alterations and additions in 1913-14 involved the construction of a new dormitory between the two buildings to create a large central dormitory which joined the cottages and created a small open court between the new dormitory and the bathroom and kitchen pavilion.

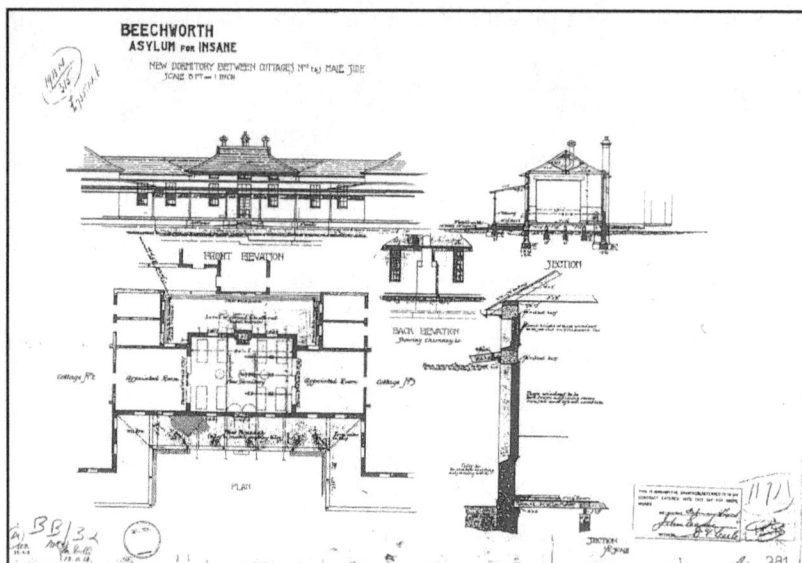

CONTRACT PLAN FOR THE 1914 JOINING OF THE TWO WARDS

Substantial alterations and additions in 1959 comprised the construction of utility rooms in the open court, the enclosing of the verandahs along the west elevation to form corridors, the construction of a dining room and day room extension at the north end of the north cottage as well as additional bathroom and laundry facilities at the south end of the south cottage.

OLIVENE LODGE (M10)

Olivene, the southern-most of the male cottages, was used to house the most dangerous male patients. Those classed as criminally-insane were here, and the building was the most secure of the cottages as a result of its occupants.

40

Dayroom - Olivene

Autopsy Table - Grevillea

Internal Courtyard - Olivene
Allowing Freedom yet still Safely Contained

℘ ⁓ ℘

McCarthy House

McCarthy House, thought to have been built in the early 1870s, is located outside the east wall along the rear entrance road and was originally used as the Medical Officer's Quarters.

The rear section, comprising the kitchen, bathroom, dining room, wash house and a bedroom, was demolished in 1960 and rebuilt. It was used by La Trobe to lease self-contained accommodation on the grounds, and its yard is bordered by some of the remaining ha-ha wall to the west.

Artisan's Buildings

To the southeast of the main building, the Artisan's Buildings contained the original stables, coach house and craftsmen's buildings, including stonemasonry and carpentry areas. The storage racks for the wooden planks still exists, and the area is now privately owned as a residence and future short-term guesthouses.

GEORGE KERFERD CLINIC/KERFERD HOTEL

Originally the George Kerferd Clinic, the building was opened in 1977. The Kerferd Clinic, which cost over $1 million to build on what was once the site of the residence of the hospital superintendent, was designed for the short-term and out-patient psychiatric care of distressed people from the region.

MORGUE/CHAPEL OF THE RESURRECTION

The original morgue was constructed in 1868 as the 'dead house', or mortuary, for the hospital. It is located west of the main building, down a steep hill and close to the western boundary of the site. The original building was a windowless, two roomed structure, toplit by a skylight.

The floor in both rooms sloped inwards from each wall to the drainage pits in the centre of the floors. It had two sets of two-leaf timber boarded doors at the north and south ends, and a central chimney for ventilation. It ceased to be used as a mortuary from 1959 when a new mortuary was constructed. The building was converted to a chapel in the 1960s.

Note: The second, most recent morgue was located at the eastern edge of the asylum, opposite the Artisans' building. It was demolished in the 2000s.

LINAKER HOTEL

Now a beautiful art deco hotel named after the landscape gardener Hugh Linaker, the former nurses hostel was built after it was decided the individual huts and single-room cottages previously used for staff were no longer suitable as the asylum grew in size.

LINAKER HOTEL, ONCE THE NURSES' HOSTEL

It was constructed in 1936-7 to the design of Public Works Department Chief Architect, Percy Everett.

Linaker is a three-storey brick and mortar-banded building with each floor featuring a central corridor with rooms both sides, and a staircase at either end of the building. The roof is a timber-framed, with overhanging eaves.

PAVILION

The Sports Pavilion, constructed in the 1910s, served as a change rooms, umpire area, and general use facility for the sporting grounds and the teams fielded by the patients and staff of the asylum.

THE PAVILLION, FOR SPORTING ACTIVITIES IN THE ASYLUM

THE PINES (INDIGO SHIRE OFFICES)

Located north of the main building overlooking the cricket oval, Turquoise Ward was designed by Percy Everett, Chief Architect of the Public Works Department, and built in 1936 as the 'New Female Ward for Congenital Mental Defectives'.

TURQUOISE WARD, NOW THE PINES, WITH ITS NAMESAKE TREES

The construction of the building, the first ward outside the containment wall, showed a change in treatment within the hospital toward what is now known as the training school function rather than the psychiatric function.

The building has three wings in a shallow 'U' shape. The central wing had day rooms and a dining room, while the two side wings provided accommodation for the patients. The design, with its broad verandahs, and open dining and common areas, was in stark contrast to that of the original asylum building.

Following its construction, it was reported that the new female ward, which was known as F9 was both comfortable and well-designed for its purpose.

It is now owned by Indigo Shire Council, and serves as the council's main offices and area of operation.

THE GATEHOUSE/GATE LODGE

The gatehouse was built at the same time as the original asylum building. It formed the main point-of-entry for the asylum and all who would visit for personal reasons or to make deliveries. There was originally a second, rear gatehouse at the start of the eastern approach to the stores are, but that is gone now.

THE GATE LODGE, VIEWED FROM INSIDE THE GROUNDS NEAR WHERE THE ROAD SPLITS TO THE FRONT AND REAR OF THE FACILITY

The contract for the works on the lodges, ha-ha and divisional walls was awarded to Abraham Linacre, who was also the contractor for the main building, at a contract price of £7,622/9/4.

In 1891, a single storey addition was made to the building, which had been converted to the Steward's Quarters in 1870. This addition was also designed by the Public Works Department.

The building was later used as the Engineer's quarters (1937-1972).

Originally the Gate lodge contained one ground floor and two first floor bedrooms, a living room (now an office) and kitchen, as well as the shed and earth closet to the rear. An additional living or dining room was constructed at the rear in the early twentieth century.

HOSPITAL FOR THE INSANE   BEECHWORTH

LODGE AT ENTRANCE GATE

FRONT ELEVATION

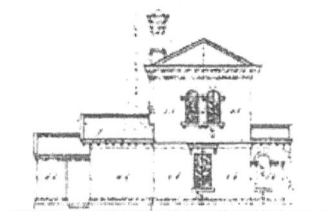

SIDE ELEVATION

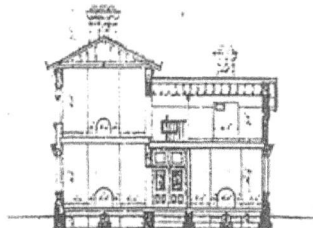

SECTION ON LINE A B

SECTION ON LINE C D

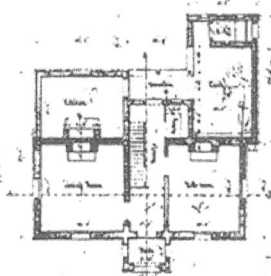

GROUND PLAN

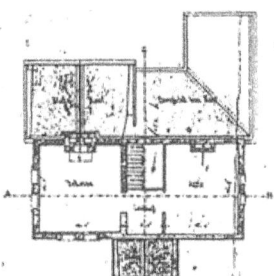

FIRST FLOOR PLAN

Further extensions were constructed relatively recently, probably in the 1970s and the original kitchen altered, in connection with the use of the building to house patients at that time

THE ORIGINAL VIEW OF THE ENTRANCE, VERY EARLY 1900S

Reasons for Admission 1867-1910

Falling off a Horse
Penniless
Orphan
Argues with Husband
Physically Deformed
Dementia
Homeless
Difficult Child
Drunkard
Excess of Opium
Kicked in the Head
Fright and Nervous Shock
Disobedient
Unmarried Mother
Prostitute
Barren
Imbecile
Fevers
Dumb
Religious Excitement
Bad Mothering
Masturbation
Change of life
Old Age
Depression
Paralysis
Uncontrolled Sexual
Appetite
Sexual Diseases
Undiagnosed Illness
Tuberculosis
Wasting Disease
Self-abuse
Incest
Overwork

Sun Stroke
Women's Afflictions
Stubbornness
Hysteria
Dropsy
Quackery
Hereditary influence
Sexual abuse
Jealousy
Immoral Life
Bloody Flux
Snuff Eating
Asthma
Greedy
Brain Fever
Laziness
Grief
Nerves
Small Pox
Novel Reading
Wearing red
Housework on Sunday
Woman in Hotel
Gunshot Wound
Egotism
Wanton Behaviour
Hard Study
Can't Speak English
Beaten
Political Excitement
Desertion by Husband
Scarlet Fever
Superstition
Hit by a Wagon
Bad Company

"a first class modern Lunatic Asylum serves quite a variety of purposes. In the popular mind it is merely a place for the isolation and safety of the dangerous. It is this; but it is also a great hygienic hospital for the restoration of the insane to physical and mental health; it is a house for moral and physical education; a school for elementary, artistic, scientific, literary, and even religious training. It is a place of numerous and orderly activities, of homely industrial occupations, where the heads and the hands of the inmates are called into systematic, healthful and daily exercise. So much has been said of late in criticism of our Victorian asylums — and I am not going to say such criticisms are uncalled for, since I am not in a position to judge — that the public, which takes but a very languid interest in these institutions, is in danger of underestimating their value to the community, and of failing to appreciate the great sanitary work that goes on silently within them.

"In the building of an asylum for the insane, two supreme objects are kept steadily in view. The first of these is to make the place as little like a prison as possible, and to carefully eliminate everything in its appearance suggestive of compulsory confinement, compatible with the safety of the inmates. The second point is to secure the best possible sanitary conditions. Both these fundamental conditions are fulfilled in a high degree at Beechworth. [E]verything from floor to ceiling was scrupulously clean — even to the very air itself. There were no superfluous articles of furniture, but everything was arranged on an intelligent plan, and with a view to combining comfort with the utmost cleanliness."

—'*A Run through the Beechworth Asylum*', 6th June, 1903, *The Ovens and Murray Advertiser*

TOURS RUN THROUGH THE OLD ASYLUM
NEARLY EVERY DAY OF THE YEAR.

- AFTER DARK HISTORY/GHOST TOURS EVERY NIGHT -
- FAMILY-FRIENDLY TWILIGHT TOURS FRI& SAT -
- PURE HISTORY EVERY SATURDAY & SUNDAY -
- PRIVATE TOURS AVAILABLE ON QUERY -

ASYLUM
GHOST TOURS
BEECHWORTH, VICTORIA
0473 376 848
WWW.ASYLUMGHOSTTOURS.COM

REFERENCES

"A Run Through the Beechworth Lunatic Asylum". (6th June, 1903). *The Ovens and Murray Advertiser*. [Accessed: 6th July, 2017. http://trove.nla.gov.au/newspaper/article/201471602]

"Beechworth Asylum. *Public Record Office Victoria*. [Accessed: 23rd June, 2016. http://www.prov.vic.gov.au]

"Beechworth Asylum". *Wikipedia*. [Accessed: 23rd June 2016. http:// https://en.wikipedia.org/wiki/Beechworth_Asylum]

"The Beechworth Lunatic Asylum". (23rd May, 1867). Supplement to the *Ovens and Murray Advertiser*. [Accessed: 22nd June, 2016. http://trove.nla.gov.au/newspaper/article/198659585]

Craig, D. A. (2000). *The Lion of Beechworth: An account of the Mayday Hills Hospital, Beechworth 1867 – 1995*.

Beechworth Lunatic Asylum. DHHS. 1996. https://www. findingrecords.dhhs.vic.gov.au/collectionresultspage/ Beechworth-Lunatic-Asylum

Lovell, Chen. (July, 2012). "Beechworth Conservation Management Plan".

www.ingramcontent.com/pod-product-compliance
Lightning Source LLC
Chambersburg PA
CBHW021146020426
42331CB00005B/915